MeAze,

Courage 2 Take The SHOT

Get In the GAME

Thanks so much for
your support. I'm so
Proud of you that you
are pursuing your love,
your pictures are beautiful.
Live life to the fullness.

Your New Friend
Debbie foreman
11/20/17
XC.

Acknowledgements

I would like to take this time to acknowledge some very special people in my life. First of all, I give GOD all the Glory in everything that I do, for truly without HIM I can do nothing.

The first special person in my life, my Husband, has been my biggest fan. He always tells me, "You can do this. You got this." You are the breath I breathe. I'm glad God choose you just for me. Love you to Life.

My twin girls, Breanna & Keanna, who are my cheerleaders, always cheering me on no matter how many times I stop and start. "Mommy, how's the book coming along?" Yes, accountability!

My Mother-in-Law who I am grateful for.

My Aunt BJ, who I can always count on to boost and uplift me any time she calls. Someone who has poured so much into my life. The women who started me on the road to broaden my horizon... I will never forget those library visits. Love You!!

My niece, Cheryl who keeps me laughing!!

I give honor and extreme thanks to Pastor Keith and Connie Moore, my Spiritual Leaders, words cannot express how you have imparted words of wisdom that have touched me and for that I will always love you and be grateful!

Debbie J. Foreman

Courage 2 Take The SHOT

Get In The GAME

ISBN 978-1540511218

Printed in the United States of America

The Book is Dedicated to my Family:

My Loving Husband- William;

My Amazing Twin daughters-

Breanna & Keanna;

My Mother-in-Law, Johnnie Mae.

Now to Him who is able to do exceedingly abundantly above all that we ask or think, according to the power that works in us.

Ephesians 3:20

<u>Table of Contents</u>

YOUR
ONLY
LIMIT
IS YOU!

Introduction

As I sit to write this book, I realized that there are women everywhere that need the Courage 2 Take the Shot. That Dream you have on the inside is bursting to come out and it's being held up by fear. Having talked to women on social media and in person, I came to the conclusion that if they had a coach or a mentor they would be more likely to take the shot.

My wish is that any woman that reads this book will find the Courage 2 Take The Shot and live the life they were truly meant to live.

I dedicate this book to my one and only sister Carol Martin, who has been my rock and supporter in everything I venture into. As my big sister she made sure to take care of me and give me wise counsel. You will forever be missed but always in my heart.

R.I.H.

Carol Martin

1961-2009

First Quarter

As a child growing up you really don't understand what your dreams mean. Once you start to realize that your dreams do mean something, you are awakened. Many times we just dream and ask other people the meaning and they give crazy answers. Of course, everyone heard I dreamed about fish and then someone screams I'm not pregnant.

Your dreams can take you to places you can only get to in your mind. When we were little we were able to dream and play Make-Believe. Some of the boys would be professional football and basketball players;

some of the girls would become a princess.

Back then, there was no better place to be than

in make-believe land. *Oh how that land was*

filled with laughter and happiness. As we grew

older some of us started journals and writing

down our dreams to make sure that we pursued

them. As time goes by and life happens we stop

dreaming, one of the dreams I use to have was

writing a book because I read so many of

Danielle Steele's Novels. She was a mom of 7

and found the time to write novel after novel. I

thought to myself if she can do it, so can I.

My dreams of being a teacher slowly faded with time growing up and realizing the children were different. The dream of modeling hit me in NJ with my auntie who broaden my horizon. After seeing Beverly Johnson grace many magazines, I just knew that was what I aspired to do.

The modeling days of running here and there, doing department stores modeling and some runway modeling was priceless. The highlight of that time for me was a fashion show where Eddie Murphy was the guest

A couple of us got to hang out with him and his friends. We laughed and danced all night. That slowly became a memory because of the demanding schedule that was put on us models.

What FEAR is Holding You BACK!!!!

_____

_____

_____

_____

_____

_____

_____

_____

Second Quarter

As the Facebook revolution came around and people started to connect with one another, a whole new world came forth. Opportunities were everywhere; you literally could pick and choose what venture you wanted. I love seeing Women Empowering Women. It's awesome seeing women uplift and not tear down each other. Women were emerging as Authors, Speakers and Branding themselves as experts. With the avalanche of negativity and drama that Facebook sometimes has going on, I decided that my posts be geared toward Positivity and Upliftment.

As I started to talk with my family and let them know that I'm interested in writing a book, they let me know that I didn't have any experience. They were worried about who's going to read what I have to say. They were my Dream Stealers and they had planted the seed of doubt. *Family believe they know what's best for you.*

Well, after receiving that blow from them I talked with my so-called friends and was also dealt a blow to my confidence as well. They told me, "What do you know? Nobody is going to read that." After that encounter, I started to believe that I *could* do it.

Then you realize that the people that are Dream Stealers, are the ones that didn't have the nerve to go after their dream. Fear stepped in and took over and they were not strong enough to fight it, but you were and now in their eyes you think you are better than them cause you fought fear and wouldn't let fear win.

You just chose Faith or fear and if you make that choice each and every time, you will win. It may be your family, it may be your friends that will steal your joy but what journey is meant for you is for you. Everyone can watch

you take it, but everyone can't go.

DO YOU HAVE THE COURAGE 2 TAKE THE SHOT?

(List your dreams here)

_____

_____

_____

_____

_____

_____

_____

_____

_____

_____

_____

Third Quarter

Since my family and friends were the Dream Stealers, it was time to take a different route, as I started to reach out to people who had done it already on Facebook. The first young lady was friendly and didn't mind answering my questions, like how long did it take you and did you self- publish. She said, "Girl, you can do it. Go for it." My confidence level went high after that conversation. The next Author I asked questions was also friendly and did not mind sharing her knowledge. She told me to take my time and make it fun. *Wow, this is a stranger*

being more supportive than friends and family.
The more and I started to immerse myself into
the community and with like-minded individual
authors, the language of "can do" started to be
the language of talk, instead of "you can't".
They assisted me in enrolling for a course that
would stir me in the right direction.

Once you realize that there is a whole
world of can do out there, not a world of that
sounds strange, don't do that my friend did it
and it didn't work or you are doing one of those
things.

The language became you can do it,

follow us on our page and any help you need let

us know, we are here to help.

Fourth Quarter

It was time for me to have the Courage 2 Take the SHOT, no longer sitting on the bench being a cheerleader. I was cheering everyone on and talking about I'm next but never taking action to make it happen. It was time to put the fear to the side and just do it. How many of you have let fear stop you from your Dreams? Procrastination can come in many forms to rob you of your Destiny.

We have been taught that our Excuses are legitimate, so we can use them and it's ok. Once you put fear aside the world is literally your oyster. I started to write and write and the words wouldn't stop. Put fear aside and let your creative bloom take charge.

Once you have been blind all your life, and now see that the possibilities are limitless you get a brand new talk and walk. You get that confident stride and hold your head up because you realize that the sky is not the limit since there are footprints on the moon.

You wake every morning with a pep in your step just knowing that you can because He did. I could have used all the excuses such as "since my mom, dad and only sister are no longer here". Or the excuse "it's time consuming", or "my job is too demanding and when I get home I'm tired". What excuse are you using that holding you back from your inner potential.

The first Shot I took was Launching an Travel Business online with no experience whatsoever. Knowing that life was meant to be lived and I thought I was living it, a occasion vacation here and there just to Myrtle Beach or Virginia Beach or somewhere in NC was just normal because that's what everyone else did.

Well this was my first introduction to MLM, Multi Level Marketing and I decided to take a SHOT because the old industrialize way of doing things were long gone and the more and more that I immerse myself into the culture and the people, I change.

The person that I was becoming and the bond with like minding individuals was breath taking. Our conversations were totally different we talked about financial future, owning property and traveling to exotic places. What a refreshing opportunity. Sometimes you have to step out of the box and do something out of the

ordinary.

Conclusion

As I began to Take the Shot, so many emotions filled me, like ""I'm really doing this" and I appreciate all the Authors who I reached out to and were truly open and honest with me. Moving to the next level is truly going to take some sacrifice. Family and friends will never understand the hustle. The grind is real because the Legacy is real. Courage 2 Take the Shot will help you find your courage, and watch your life unfold in front of you.

Today, I take the Shot to become an

Author because one day my grandkids will ask,

"Was there anything you wanted to do, nanna

that you didn't?" I want the answer to be no. It's

time for you to take the shot. What fear is

holding you back?

There's a Business Owner on the Inside!

There's an Author on the Inside!

There's a Chef on the Inside!

There's an Event Planner on the Inside!

There's a _____ *on*

the Inside!

Fill in the blank.

DO YOU HAVE THE COURAGE 2 TAKE

THE SHOT?

CALL TO ACTION

Some people will read this book and not be effected at all then there will be those that read it and say thanks I really needed to hear that. See we need to guard what we see and what we hear, cause negativity can creep in like a thief in the night to still your joy and creativity that's on the inside of you. So yes Now, Right NOW this is your CALL TO ACTION – What Are You going to DO!!

About the Author

Debbie has an unwavering desire and dedication to Empower as many women as possible so they can have the Courage 2 Take the Shot and live the life they were meant to have.

Debbie loves her husband and family and the awesome people in her life. She loves vacationing with her family, especially Cruising on the Carnival Cruise Line. One of her favorite destinations is Nassau, Bahamas!!

What's your next Destination? Let me help you create memories. Go to www.2twinstravel.com and let the venture begin.

Network Marketing was my first step toward taking the Courage 2 Take The Shot, with the low overhead what did I have to lose. As I prayed to God that there had to be more to life than work and sleep and doing the same thing over and over, a magazine came to my house that changed my life.

Network Marketing has given me life in the form of Personal Development and Bonding with like minded People. Most of which I would have never ever met before. This Industry is awesome because ordinary people become extraordinary individuals with this personal development that is not taught in school. I have become a avid reader and my library at home is living proof. You have family and friends who criticise the industry because they have no clue about the industry.

I'm a part of the Travel Industry and my host agency is Xstream Travel. This company has allowed me and my family to travel for the very first time on a cruise. Travel which is the largest industry in the world. The memories that me and my family have made is because of this company and those are priceless and I am forever grateful.

I can be contact below:

Email – debbiejoynerforeman@gmail.com

FB – facebook.com/debbieforeman.35

Instagram- debbieforeman35

TAKE

THE

SHOT

You must remain focus on

your

JOURNEY

To

GREATNESS

44058473R00025

Made in the USA
Middletown, DE
26 May 2017